A History of Broken

A History of Broken

Trevor Church

napalm press   los angeles

Copyright © 2021 by Trevor Church

All rights reserved

ISBN: 978-0-578-32425-8

www.TrevorChurch.com

Cataloging-in-Publication Data

Names: Church, Trevor, 1991-author.

Title: A history of broken/ Trevor Church

Description: Los Angeles : Napalm Press, 2021.

Subjects: 1. Young men – Poetry. 2. Gay men –
Poetry. 3. LGBTQ – Poetry. 4. English language –
History. 5. History – Language.

We're all born to broken people on their most honest day of living. Listener, *Wooden Heart*

The world breaks everyone and afterward many are strong at the broken places. Ernest Hemingway, *A Farewell to Arms*

American society, literary or lay, tends to be humorless. What other culture could have produced someone like Hemingway and not seen the joke? Gore Vidal, *Edmund Wilson: This Critic and This Gin and These Shoes*

For Anna Nicole, Marilyn, and all the other people we broke beyond repair.

1. I recently learned that a broken heart is a real thing, medically. I fact checked what I found with Harvard Medical School, the Mayo Clinic, and good ol' WebMD. I was astonished. It's real. What I'm feeling has been validated. The medical term is Takotsubo Cardiomyopathy. It can be caused by extreme emotions.

2. Although rare, Takotsubo Cardiomyopathy can be lethal.

3. It is entirely possible to die of a broken heart.

4. This revelation has given a great deal of credibility to every poet I've ever read. My sincerest apologies to Dylan Thomas for the harsh criticisms I wrote in the margins of his books during my undergrad.

5. The name comes from the Japanese word for an octopus trap. The trap has a narrow path, followed by a bulbous bottom. This shape is similar to the left ventricle of the heart that begins to narrow during Takotsubo Cardiomyopathy.

6. The condition can affect anyone, men or women. Although, it affects women more often.

7. I think this means women feel more. Or care more.

8. When I read this, I thought of the Alice Cooper song "Only Women Bleed."

9. I was also reminded of the Princess Diana quote where she says she would like to lead with the heart, not the head. I think she did, and I think maybe it killed her. Society views the heart as a dangerous thing.

10. It's fitting while working on this project, I suffered from heartbreak for the first time in years. I'm using my broken pieces for kindling here with sick satisfaction. While doing so, the specific kind of dread that can only come from self-awareness hit me: do I self-sabotage for the sake of writing material? Has every fuck-up been in the name of art? Maybe not. But now I have an excuse that makes me sound more intellectual than I am when in conversation with my therapist, or the dreadful husband of a distant acquaintance at my heartbreakers next Christmas party.

11. Yes, I'll still go. I'll write to you about it after. I always seem to intentionally pour salt in the wound.

12. Has my left ventricle narrowed?

13. Does it narrow over a lifetime or is it one good break that causes it to narrow?

14. Around 30% of people with Takotsubo Cardiomyopathy can't identify a cause. This leads me to believe their heartbreak is the slow burning kind. A lifetime accumulation from fractures to the heart before it finally breaks. But if this is true, every marginalized person would die from it surely. Or perhaps their arteries have hardened to the point they can't narrow. Maybe they are better equipped to deal with the breaks.

15. The first known use of the word broken was in the 13th century. The word has since transformed a bit, but the meaning has remained the same. Nothing else could describe the feeling in all of its anguish except broke. A simple word in pronunciation, with a hard emphasis on the K. broKUH.

16. The first use of broke in the financial sense was in 1593 by Shakespeare "The Kings growne bankrupt like a broken man." Shortly after, broke became synonymous with poor. In more ways than one.

17. It took its current form, broken, in the times of Middle English. In Old English it was brocen. From Proto-Germanic brukanaz, a cognate with dutch gebroken, or the German gebrochen.

18. Your drunk uncle Scotty can now blame broken hearts on Western Europe, like he does with most other things at Thanksgiving.

19. The meaning of the word has virtually stayed the same, as I mentioned. "That which breaks, affliction, misery."

20. Same shit, different century.

21. "You're too broken to be in a relationship. I don't want to break you more than you already are, and eventually I will." He said.

22. That was the day I inadvertently began writing this book. I thought he sounded like one of those

inspirational pictures one finds on Tumblr or Pinterest. It was just him repeating something he saw on social media. It made me cringe on his behalf. And what the hell did broken mean anyways? I'd been seeing the word in a noticeable incline lately. It was in book titles, films, songs, used by therapists. It wasn't just a term that became trendy on the internet. The word began to take on a new life. When, I'm not sure. But I started jotting down a note whenever I saw the word in use outside of typical settings.

23. "Too broken." This would imply I can't be fixed. This leads me to two conclusions with great juxtaposition:

a. Everything and everyone is "too broken" in comparison to their original state of being.

b. "Too broken" is an impossible state. Nothing is broken beyond repair.

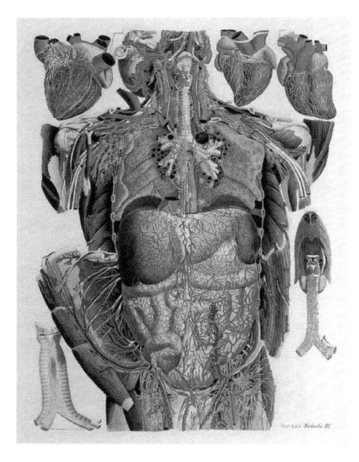

24. Recently, I've been going through old encyclopedias whenever I can find them and looking at old medical drawings. Whenever I find

one of a broken limb, and their practice of mending it, I make a copy of the photograph. Most medical practices prior to this century seem barbaric and torturous. Methods for fixing broken limbs is no different. The giant wooden splints secured to patients who are secured to a board are hardly comforting. But they did what they thought would help. Maybe that's what you were doing? Just doing what you thought would help.

25. Like most things, the history of healing fractured bones goes back to ancient Egypt, where they used bark wrapped in fabric to create a splint.

26. Like most things, the history of healing fractured bones has to mention Hippocrates, who recommended wooden splints and exercise for fractured bones as methods to heal. This isn't far off from today: a cast, and physical therapy.

27. In Greece they used fabric dipped in wax and resin. In Rome they used starch to harden fabric, and lime and egg whites were used by Arabian doctors. Other mixtures came about using mixtures of these ingredients, and things like flour, before the French surgeon Ambroise Pare began making casts from wax, cardboard, fabric, and parchment.

28. In 1812, Dominque Jean Larrey (also a Frenchman) worked as a military doctor. One of his patients had to have his arm amputated after the Battle of Borodino. The wound was covered, and the patient was slowly transported from Russia to France. By the time he reached France, the wound from the procedure had healed. The doctor then concluded wounds need to be covered. He started covering the wounds of all patients with stiffened bandages.

29. Note: consider time and bandages for nursing heart.

30. The practices of how we treat broken things has continued to improve. We also have oxycontin now, so there's that. I considered that for my heart but figured it was a slippery slope.

31. Eventually, a man named Nikolay Pirogov introduced what is now known as the modern cast (although this is debated). Hospitals handmade the bandages until 1931 when commercial bandages called Cellona were produced in Germany.

32. Returning to item #29, I wonder how well time and plaster casting will work on my heart, or myself

as an individual, since I've been called broken. How much fiberglass, polyurethane, and cotton will I have to ingest or perhaps stuff into my rectum before my heart is protected and can heal. I could probably smoke a cigarette: I'm sure they also contain those ingredients. I would assume my heart is more at risk in this fragile state, although the medical encyclopedias offer nothing other than the suggested use of SSRI's. But that dulls the pain, it doesn't let the wound heal necessarily. Smoking a cigarette would also probably be a slippery slope.

33. Nikolay Pirogov has been dead a long time and forgot to leave us a treatment plan for the shattered heart.

34. His body remains untouched and preserved in a church in Vinnytsia, Ukraine (a town still haunted by the mass execution of 11,000 people by the Nazis in 1938). A technique he invented was used to preserve the body perfectly. It requires the occasional dusting, but that's it. Perhaps, had he dedicated the amount of time to broken hearts that he dedicated to preserving his post-mortem vanity, we wouldn't be so broken. Admittedly, it is impressive that a man found a way to ensure he

wouldn't break, even after death. His corpse looks porcelain.

35. I considered traveling to Vinnytsia and holding a séance next to his body to see if he had any broken heart tips to share, since he cured broken limbs and decomposition. I tried to reach the church and ask for permission. I even told them my last name is church. I received no response. I also thought about contacting his descendants, but I realized the risk in being deemed crazy. Then I would be both crazy and broken. Crazy – a concept that's been used against my broken heart too many times.

36. I come from a broken home. I'm not sure who first told me this or when I first realized it. As outdated as the term is, by definition it can be applied to my single-parent upbringing. The term was first used between 1840 and 1850. This is when broken began to branch further from its literal definition.

37. I was able to reach a man in Ukraine. Although his *broken English* was superb, I couldn't properly convey holding a séance next to a porcelain dead person. I've thought on my approach and still

cannot find a better way to articulate my wants. That wasn't an issue with us. I was very clear about my wants.

38. Ellen Lupton wrote an article for The New York Times titled "In Praise of the Broken Home." She traced the phrase to its origins and through its evolution. After its initial application for families abandoned by a member or a member dying, it was used by the temperance movement to describe families affected by alcoholism.

39. Ellen Lupton admits in the article she too comes from a broken home. I thought about contacting her to see what her thoughts on a broken heart are.

40. Okay, I've contacted her. Her article is beautiful, and I wanted to tell her, but didn't ask about broken hearts.

41. In the article, Ellen Lupton concludes "this home has been broken, but I don't try to fix it. The cracks and gashes have made it what it is."

42. Lupton has concluded the broken things are not meant to be fixed – they are beautiful and their own

entity, separate from what they were before they broke.

43. I agree with this to an extent, but I left a broken heart unattended once and ended up on a combination of Welbutrin, Lamictal, Adderall, Klonopin, and Lexapro. I got better when I finally addressed the places it was broken. The other time I ignored what was broken, I was left with a temporarily deformed face, and a permanent third dimple.

44. I was seven and jumping on the bed to Weird Al's "I'm Fat" with a pillow stuffed in my shirt. The son of my dad's friend was doing the same, when he body slammed me like a sumo wrestler. I flew off the bed, my face going into the corner of a coffee table, and the cheekbone breaking. My father was too drunk to drive to the hospital. Ice was applied. A week later when my mom picked me up, it was still swollen, purple, and mangled. At that point anything a doctor could do would be cosmetic. Eventually the swelling went down. So did the visits with my father. A month or so later, a third dimple was left where the split in the bone is. When I smile you can see it. Visibly broken.

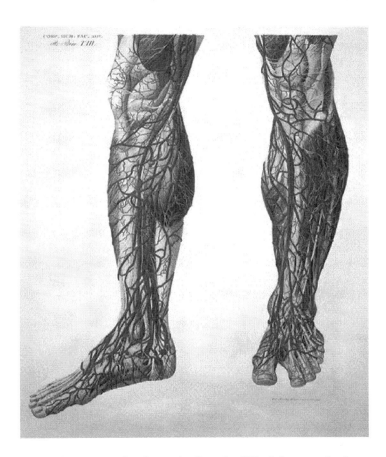

45. A bone was broken. A dimple filled the crack. Is my third dimple the result of a broken bone or a

broken home? If we are to listen to Lupton, my broken bone and the third dimple in its place are perhaps beautiful. A quote frequently misattributed to Marilyn Monroe "imperfections are beauty" would suggest my dimple is beautiful.

46. I'm not sure who actually said that, but I know it wasn't Marilyn.

47. My cheekbone had been broken. Broken like the coffee table you once pushed me over, or my bedroom door that you shoved me through. Broken like our relationship and my heart after the later. I never got around to fixing that door before I moved.

48. While broken bones are freshly on my mind, I'd like to take a second to discuss the phrase "break a leg."

49. It's unfortunate news I must tell you... "break a leg" is an idiom that is now considered a dead metaphor.

50. In other words, its origins are completely lost. I was very disappointed by this and understand if you are too. I had hoped for some great story where someone broke their leg during an audition and still

got the part, and that part transformed their life for the better. Let's just pretend this is the case.

51. There is some speculation about the origin of "break a leg" that I will share with you.

52. In his 1918 autobiography Manfred von Richthofen, a German fighter pilot in WWI, records the phrase "Hals- und beinbruch" as something pilots said to each other before flight. It translates to "neck and leg break" and was meant as a way to say good luck. Why and how this phrase came to be, no one can say. It has been hypothesized to come from the Hebrew phrase "hatzlacha u-bracha" because the two sound similar. That phrase comes from Yiddish "hatsloche un broche" which means success and blessing. Break a leg in a way is a positive way to reclaim what's broken.

53. Perhaps fighter pilots said it because they hoped to break the necks and legs of enemies. Though morbid, this wouldn't surprise me. After all, we use violent phrases like this to wish each other luck: telling boxers to knock one another out, "kick their ass" is something we yell at athletes as they take the field. So, we regard broken as a good thing when its someone other than ourselves that's breaking.

54. Wishing others harm, and to break, brings me to my next point of origin: horse racing. Robert Lynd published "A Defence [sic] of Superstition" in 1921 for the magazine New Statesman. He exclaimed it's unlucky to wish someone luck, but instead you should insult them or say something mean such as "may you break your leg." I wish instead of breaking my heart, you followed Robert Lynd's lead and just broke my leg. It would've been much less painful.

55. How did Yiddish slang make its way from German fighter pilots to NYC theaters? It's assumed by many to have been brought over by Jewish immigrants who entered the entertainment industry after the war.

56. The term became popular enough by the 1940's that it began appearing in print. In Edna Ferber's autobiography from 1939, she writes "all of the understudies sitting in the back row politely wishing the various principals would break a leg."

57. One theory I'll share, that's completely false, is the Abraham Lincoln theory. Although disproven, I want to share it because it's exactly the type of

origin story I was hoping for. I was sorely let down. So let's pretend this is how it happened.

58. The assassin actor, John Booth, who killed Lincoln, claimed in a diary he broke his leg leaping the stage when trying to rush out of the theater after shooting Lincoln. Unfortunately, Booth was a liar and liked to greatly exaggerate in his diaries. Had he been telling the truth, one might also consider the broken leg bad luck, since although he got away via horse, he was killed two weeks later.

59. Maybe the luck from a broken leg is temporary, like there's a two week cap on it. Similarly, when you break a mirror, there is also a cap, but not on good luck, on bad luck. The cap is seven years. Seems a little unfair though (bad luck usually is): a broken legs gives you two solid weeks of good and a broken mirror gives you seven shit years.

60. How many mirrors did I break to deserve this?

61. Fortunately for you, the origins of a broken mirror causing back luck are more easily traced than the origins of "break a leg." Although, maybe that gives them more merit, which should frighten all of us – especially the clumsy.

62. Bad luck stemming from a broken mirror dates back thousands of years to the Greeks and Romans. The romans were the first to actually manufacture mirrors and believed the gods used them to look at our souls. Anyone reckless enough to break a mirror would surely offend the gods, who would then curse them with bad luck.

63. The belief the bad luck caused by a broken mirror lasts seven years is almost as old as the mirrors themselves. Israel Drazin wrote in Maimonides and the Biblical Prophets the Romans believed the body to renew itself every seven years. It's likely they believed we renewed ourselves and became void of bad luck after the renewal process, in this case, seven years. Seven years for a broken mirror.

64. Not to worry, if you are reading this book because you have broken a mirror and cannot handle the seven-year waiting period on ancient curses, there might be a solution.

65. I found a list online containing methods to rid yourself of the seven-year curse cast by the broken mirror. I wondered as I read the list *could these work for a broken heart?*

- Throw salt over your left shoulder
- Spin in a circle three times
- Grind the mirror into a fine powder
- Reuse the broken mirror
- Toss the broken mirror into a south running stream (don't do this, even if your luck is bad, please, think of the environment)
- Blacken the mirror with fire
- Touch a tombstone with one glass shard

66. I threw the salt, I spun, I couldn't grind my heart into powder since you already did but I tore up your picture. I could try to reuse it if only I could figure out how. I swam in a south running stream, strolled through a graveyard, and blackened it with time and the nightly news. I guess I just have to wait seven years.

67. The song Cecilia and the Satellites by Andrew McMahon in the Wilderness always grabs my attention. One verse specifically: "crashed my car, I was seventeen/My mother in the seat right next to me/The things I've learned from a broken mirror/How a face can change when a heart knows fear." As of lately, this verse has been sticking with me more than ever. I have to pause the song and

think on it. My first thought goes to the broken mirror – obviously. I wonder if McMahon had bad luck after it. Or perhaps the bad luck started before, and that's why he wrecked and broke perhaps another mirror. I decided to look up his year of birth, found out he would've been seventeen in 1999, so I examined his career between 1999 and 2006. Seven years. He was in a band called Something Corporate during these years. They made a few albums and EP's, and had a following. They were successful in an incredibly competitive industry. It would seem he didn't have any outwardly bad luck from the mirror. I was almost disappointed when I read this.

68. I can't recall if I've ever broken a mirror.

69. Maybe the person he crashed his car into had bad luck for seven years… like they absorbed his during the collision. I have no way of finding out for sure though. My next thought goes to what this verse could be saying about his relationship with his mother. Is it a metaphor? Was the car crash and broken mirror representative of a personal problem they had? Is broken literal or metaphorical here? Maybe it's both. Maybe every broken thing is always both. I'm starting to believe this.

70. When my heart breaks, there is the obvious figurative aspect, but the pain in my chest coming from anxiety makes me believe the broken object is also literal. Takotsubo cardiomyopathy?

71. Cecilia isn't the first song that pops into my head when I think of broken in the context of music. Surprisingly, I think of Jack Johnson's catalogue. In high school I had a girlfriend, Laurel, who would drive us around in her red Honda. She had a love for Jack Johnson. It was through her I came to know his music, and why broken is engraved next to him in my head, and now her. He has two songs specifically: Broken and Breakdown. In Broken he sings "without you I was broken/But I'd rather be broke down with you by my side" implying we are incomplete people, and to function properly we must find the person who is the missing piece to our appliance. I don't think I agree with this.

72. Breakdown resonated with me more. "I hope this old train breaks down/Then I could take a walk around/See what there is to see/Time is just a melody." He is either referring to life as a train ride where we are just a passenger, or our life rhythm and selves are the train. Either way, he needs the

ride to stop so he can truly appreciate what's around him.

73. Did my heart need to get broken so I could love better? Or better yet, did it need to break so I could fix it, and find myself in doing so? Maybe I needed to breakdown. Maybe that's what McMahon meant by the things he learned from a broken mirror – he saw things individually in the shards. If life is just shards of a mirror, how many of my pieces cast your reflection?

74. I was talking to a man possibly high on methamphetamine at the bus stop. He asked me what I'm working on now. I said a book about broken things. He said things are supposed to be broken. If they weren't, we wouldn't exist.

75. "What do you mean?" I asked, while wondering why I was asking. Sometimes I really can't stop myself.

76. "Pangea. Who knows if we would exist had it not happened." As sleep deprived as this man probably was, I spent the rest of the day thinking about Pangea.

77. Pangea was a giant continent made up of all of the continents. It began to divide and break apart 175 million years ago. Pangea comes from ancient Greek, meaning pan (whole) and Gaia (mother earth). Pangea is the whole mass of land on earth. The concept of Pangea originated in 1912 when Alfred Wegener published The Origin of Continents.

78. Pangea is now widely accepted by geologists. Back then, it was just a theory. Was the breakup of Pangea necessary for life as we know it, or would humans have eventually evolved on the giant mass? It turns out the man from the bus stop is right. Life came from the broken pieces.

79. The lack of diverse landscapes in Pangea essentially favored certain species.

80. There were three major phases in the breakup of Pangea, as there was in the breaking of my heart.

81. Phase one: the Atlantic Ocean began to form when Africa and North America began to split. "I'm busy this weekend, and next. I'll call you."

82. Phase two: Africa, South America, India, Antarctica, and Australia began to drift apart. "I just need some space. I care about you a lot"

83. Phase three: Australia split from Antarctica, and the Atlantic and Indian Oceans continued expanding. "This just isn't working out."

84. Currently Australia and eastern Asia are drifting towards each other at a pace of 2-3 inches a year. One day the broken things will collide again. Maybe I'll see you at the bus stop or in a doctor's office someday. Or your Christmas party this December. Will it be as disastrous as it will be when Australia cand eastern Asia crash into each other? Will we cause tsunamis and earthquakes?

85. "This is the last day of our acquaintance/I will meet you later in somebody's office/I'll talk but you won't listen to me/I know what your answer will be" -Sinead O'Connor

86. "Don't step on a crack or you'll break your mother's back." I want to return to broken bones again, mostly because of this rhyme. I'd forgotten about it until I heard a friend's child chanting it as he skipped with us to the store. As a child, I truly

believed stepping on a crack in the sidewalk would harm my mother. The thought terrified me. I never wondered why there was a correlation between cement cracks and my mother, or how my actions separate of her could break her physically. Nonetheless, I was so scared. I remember the rhyme eating away at me. It dominated my thoughts whenever I wasn't safely on carpet. There was probably a solid year where I was unable to walk a straight line – always avoiding the broken places.

87. I had quite a few eccentricities as a child. I told my psychiatrist this. She said "almost all kids have obsessive tendencies. That's very normal." Being conditioned to fear what is broken is normal.

88. Unfortunately, just like the ice cream truck song, I discovered the origins of this rhyme are racist. It became widely used in the late 19th century. "Don't step on a crack or your mother's baby will be black" or other but similarly grotesque versions were recited, before it transformed to the version we know today.

89. Is there anything in this country that doesn't stem from racism? Probably not. Nothing is sacred.

90. I suppose that's what happens when you steal land through genocide and then build a country with slave labor. A broken country.

91. A broken country/government is also referred to as a failed state. This is often used to describe a country whose government has essentially dissolved. Criticism of the term says it is overused and used as an excuse to justify military intervention. I recently heard broken government applied to the US as a result of the damage the republican party has done to the country. I thought *although they have done some shitty things, does that classify the entire country as broken?* I have heard the term recently applied to Syria and Afghanistan. Perhaps the US is a broken country but that seems drastic when compared to current events in Syria. As I said in my last point, it was built on the genocide of indigenous people and with slave labor.

92. Those indigenous to the area have however fought to reclaim and rebuild what has been broken. One of their many efforts was even called "Trail of Broken Treaties." It was a four-mile-long protest that made its way from the West Coast to Washington D.C. Over 200 tribes participated from

twenty-five states. The caravan demanded restoration of tribes' treaty-making authority, federal assistance, and the abolishment of the Bureau of Indian Affairs. John Trudell, the famous Indigenous activist, participated and helped orchestrate the protest. This was before he dated Angelina Jolie's mom, and before his family was possibly murdered by the government. A documentary on his life, which features a segment on the caravan, called Trudell, was made in 2005. I watched it in my quest to make a list of broken things. The documentary starts off with a speech that proclaims it is a "society of broken promises." With that one word starting off the documentary, broken, I knew I would gather things I needed to write about.

93. Trudell believed our society broken. What about the government and country?

94. He implies these things are broken too but didn't specifically say in the documentary. He speaks with such conviction and defiance. I have no choice but to believe the words he does say. Kind of like I did with you: I believed everything.

95. I realized this evening instead of agonizing in bed for an hour about having to get out of bed to turn off the light, I can simply reach up and pull the cord hanging from the ceiling fan to turn it off without actually leaving bed. I've lived here for a year and just realized it. Maybe a year from now I will realize something so obvious and in front of me about all of the broken things, including my heart, and say "duh." One can only hope.

96. A proper response to a broken heart should always be "duh."

97. In 2016, Melissa Hill wrote a beautiful article titled "Can Tylenol Help Heal a Broken Heart?" where she outlines experience alongside research done showing acetaminophen (the active ingredient in Tylenol) can in fact reduce our neuroresponses that stem from heartache. I wonder if Hill has tried this in the years since she wrote the article, and if it worked. I might reach out and ask her.

98. I just took a Tylenol.

99. In response to Hill's article, Samier Mansur wrote "No, Tylenol Won't Heal Your Broken Heart, But This Might..." Mansur agrees research does

show it could help, but she counters that it will dull all emotions – as if this is a negative.

100. She goes on to highlight one study showing people who take painkillers are 20% less happy. This is probably because they're in pain. She argues with the Rumi quote "the cure for pain, is in the pain." She adds to this by saying "when mending a broken heart, we have two choices: dwell in it, or move forward." This reminds me of when I suffered my first bout of depression. Friends would say to me "just get out in nature, go on a walk, try yoga." Would you tell a person with a broken leg to run a marathon?

101. No (see item #28).

102. I think of one scene in the film Practical Magic, where Sandra Bullock is so brokenhearted over her husband dying, she can't leave bed. She doesn't eat. She doesn't shower. She moves in with relatives and forgets (or neglects) her parental duties. Dulling the emotion might be the only option while we try to move forward. It might be what gets us out of bed.

103. I've taken another Tylenol.

104. I wonder if Hill has watched Practical Magic, or if she envisioned scenes like this one while writing her article. My mind right now is a mosaic of these scenes.

105. "Easy on your liver with that stuff" one friend warns in response to my Tylenol taking.

106. I'd rather face jaundice than this.

107. A mosaic after all is a broken thing. It's sometimes thousands of broken things placed together to make a photo. A mosaic makes use of the broken things. A mosaic wouldn't exist without the broken things. If nothing ever broke, no mosaics would exist outside of the ones made of pebbles on old kitschy boardwalks. The oldest mosaics date back to the 3rd millennium BC in Mesopotamia. One of the earliest mosaics discovered to still be in pristine condition is The Beauty of Durrës in Albania. It's a 97 sq ft portrait of a beautiful woman. A beautiful, broken woman.

108. "Mosaic broken hearts." -Taylor Swift

109. "To all the women and especially the young women who put their faith in this campaign and in me, I want you to know that nothing has made me prouder than to be your champion. Now, I know, I know we have still not shattered that highest and hardest glass ceiling, but someday, someone will." - Hillary Clinton said in 2016 when conceding. I watched this on television as another part of me broke inside.

110. In 2008 she said "although we weren't able to shatter that highest, hardest glass ceiling this time, thanks to you, it's got about 18 million cracks in it and the light is shining through like never before, filling us all with the hope and the sure knowledge that the path will be a little easier next time."

111. The glass ceiling she is referring to is the social barrier preventing women from succeeding. Sometimes, it's good to break things. "There's a glass ceiling to break/There's money to make/And now it's time to speed it up cause I can't move at this pace." -Lily Allen

112. A similar term was first used in 1839 by French author George Sand (pen name for Amantine Lucile Aurore Dupin) in her play Gabriel.

"Une voûte de cristal impénétrable." An impenetrable crystal vault. The term we currently know was first coined in 1978 by Marianne Schriber and Katherine Lawrence, and was used in a speech later that year by Marilyn Loden.

113. Sometimes, it's good to break things.

114. Rachel Platten sang the song Fight Song, which became the unofficial theme song for the 2016 Democratic National Convention. A year after Hillary conceded (see item #109), Rachel wrote another song: Broken Glass. "I'm gonna dance on broken glass/And I'm gonna make that ceiling crash/So what? Still got knives in my back/So what? So I'm tied to the tracks/I'm gonna dance on broken glass."

115. It reminded me of the lyrics to Annie Lennox's 1992 song Walking on Broken Glass. Although, only the titles are similar. Annie's song isn't about the glass ceiling; it's about a bad breakup. Regardless, Annie has shattered many ceilings in her own right.

116. Scott Tucker translated various sonnets from Federico Garcia Lorca. One titled Sonnet of the

Garland of Roses stopped me. "But hurry, let's entwine ourselves as one, our mouth broken, our soul bitten by love, so time discovers us safely destroyed." Is our mouth broken when conjoined? Are our words unnecessary when we have each other? Can we be safely destroyed and is it a good thing? Should we want this? Do I want this? If giving one my mouth makes ours broken, then I was already broken before my heart was. Maybe he means a broken mouth because we are not talking. In that case, there are many instances in which I wish I am broken, but unfortunately am not.

117. "You are damaged and broken and unhinged. But so are shooting stars and comets." Poet Nikita Gill writes. *Is it good to be a comet?* I thought. After all, a comet may be broken, but that broken piece is possibly responsible for the extinction of dinosaurs and perhaps our inevitable extinction. At some point do we all become comets destroying whatever is in our path? Is this the result of being broken? Or is it the result of a personality disorder? Perhaps I'm both/have both of these things. Maybe you do too. Australia and eastern Asia are broken things that will one day collide, breaking more things, like a comet. Do all broken things break

more things? Perhaps when you're broken you've become conditioned to break.

118. "He's the prettiest thing/We got the same disorder."-The Distillers

119. I did read A Million Little Pieces before the controversary surrounding it blew up. Before the controversary, and long before I started writing this, I underline the passage "The Young Man came to the Old Man seeking counsel. I broke something, Old Man. How badly is it broken? It's in a million little pieces. I'm afraid I can't help you. Why? There's nothing you can do. Why? It can't be fixed. Why? It's broken beyond repair. It's in a million little pieces." James Frey, the author, eventually came under harsh scrutiny as the book had been marketed as a true story, and parts were eventually revealed to be embellished or fabricated. His memoir and career seemed to be broken into a million pieces like the title, but he recovered and released a series of successful books, although I read recently he's facing criticism for another scandal.

120. Did the book break him? Was it true, and he already was broken into a million pieces? I don't

blame him for his first controversary. I think the core and essence of the book are true. I think he meant what he wrote. I think it reads like it's been written by a broken person. I think it's true he's in a million pieces, and I think most of us who read it are too. But I read it before I was. Was it a self-fulfilling prophecy?

121. Like most unfavorable adjectives, broken was often used to describe women until recent times (see hysterical, dramatic, etc.). Words like these were used to make women fearful of being honest. Don't get me wrong, I'm not saying this doesn't happen anymore. To show a "broken" woman, The Queen's Gambit showed a woman drinking alcohol in her underwear and displayed it like it was supposed to be the most horrendous thing on earth. The thought! Tolstoy wrote "Doctoring her seemed to her as absurd as putting together the pieces of a broken vase. Her heart was broken. Why would they try to cure her with pills and powders?" (Anna Karenina)

122. Tolstoy implies we can't fix a broken heart with pills.

123. Did he try Tylenol?

124. The other implication is the most important though: what is broken cannot be fixed. Leave it be.

125. I read Pete Doherty from the Libertines said "broken glass is just like glitter, isn't it?" I couldn't find where he said it though, or if he actually did. I saw it on one of those allegedly inspirational memes where it's a quote over a stock photo of somewhere tropical. Regardless of my opinion on those memes, I liked the quote. It also, maybe, implies we shouldn't fix broken things. They shimmer like glitter or comets. I imagined that's how Pete approached life – a true pirate like Keith Richards, ready to go out in a blaze of glory. I was almost disappointed to see he's sobered up, gotten in a serious relationship, and chilled out.

126. At some point in collecting broken things, I've gotten in the rhythm of being coherent amidst heartbreak.

127. I was watching the Unbreakable trilogy recently for inspiration. In the second film, Split, James McAvoy's character says "You are different from the rest. Your heart is pure! Rejoice! The broken are the more evolved. Rejoice." Is to be broken the antithesis of the saying "ignorance is

bliss"? Have we simply seen the world for what it is? If so, to be broken is a good thing. Like breaking open a geode perhaps.

128. Annette Bening says in 20th Century Women "Having your heart broken is a tremendous way to learn about the world." It seems on some level her character would agree with McAvoy's.

129. "Take these broken wings and learn to fly." Paul McCarney, *Blackbird.* I once bought a collection of Paul McCartney lyrics specifically for this song. It wasn't until years later when I learned what it is about: the blackbird is symbolic for a black girl. McCartney heard the call of a blackbird in Rishikesh, India and the sound stayed with and inspired him. Later in Scotland, McCartney was playing around on his guitar, thinking about the civil rights movement in the US and thought about the whole idea of "you were only waiting for this moment to arise." The moment was the civil rights movement. So, he began to write the song. By McCartney's definition and symbolism of broken in this song, it's either implied we are already broken but must learn to thrive in this condition, and/or society. In this case, white supremacy, breaks people down and they must use that as a tool to fly.

Neither interpretation implies broken a bad thing necessarily.

130. In Angie, Geena Davis proclaims "we are all broken. Those of us who are less broken need to help those who are more broken." I could agree with this but what is the litmus test for broken? How broke is too broke to help and how broken is really only a fracture that gives you a social obligation to help? And what if the less broken is the breaker? Is that the situation in my case?

131. A collection of carefully curated vinyl sits on my shelf. The smell of the mildew and dust penetrates my nostrils whenever I remove them from their cardboard sleeves, open their gatefolds, and run my fingers over the decaying artwork and portraits inside. Tapestry, Blue, Private Dancer, Rocket to Russia, Zeppelin III, Sticky Fingers, the White Album... The portrait of George Harrison inside gives me a concerning look. On side 3 of the double LP there's a scratch causing the needle on the turntable to skip: a broken record.

132. A broken record is now a phrase used to describe someone repeating themselves. Although dated (streaming is the most popular form of music

currently), most people still know what this means. Conversational anaphora. It came from a literal broken record that repeats the same part of the song over and over as the result of a scratch.

133. Not all broken records are physically broken, and not all metaphorical records are broken in the sense of repetition.

134. I have many broken records: For Emma (Bon Iver), Brothers (The Black Keys), Cannibal (Kesha). Cannibal was playing when I was in a terrible car wreck and rolled across a highway. Like McMahon (see item #67), I too was in a car wreck at seventeen, but I didn't learn anything from the broken mirror other than I can no longer listen to Kesha while driving without having a panic attack.

135. I saw The Black Keys on their tour promoting Brothers right after I graduated high school in a small venue that only held a couple hundred people. I was in the front row pressed against the railing. It was one of the best nights of my life. One of the girls I went with, one of my best friends, died tragically a few years later. Whenever I hear that record, I think of her. It's broken now.

136. For Emma was the anthem for a friend and I as we would drive around in the snow and talk about everything for hours, and not tell any of our other friends or families where we were. For awhile we even invented a fake friend named Debby, and we would tell people we were hanging out with her. It was a secret world. Whenever I hear its soothing, snow filled tracks I think of those days and the broken friendship that followed, and how no matter how hard I tried, it was unrepairable. Some broken things can't be fixed, which is really unfortunate because sometimes those broken things eat away at us daily. For Emma has eaten away at my broken pieces every day for years now. A broken record for broken parts. The album actually discusses this in a strange coincidence. "And now all your love is wasted/And then who the hell was I?/And I'm breaking at the breaches/And at the end of all your lines."

137. I feel like I live in a graveyard of broken things.

138. The straw that broke the camels back. An idiom dating back to the 1600's. The idiom describes a major action as the result of the accumulation of small actions. In the mid 1600's

the philosopher Thomas Hobbes wrote "in such Manner as the last Feather may be said to break a Horses Back, when there were so many laid on before as there want but that one to do it." It eventually became camel in 1799 (at least in the Western World, it's possible it was used earlier in China). The Scots Magazine, in issue 61, in 1799, listed "oriental proverbs," one of them is "It is the last straw that overloads the camel." It became broken and not overloaded in 1832 when Henry Lee wrote in An Exposition of Evidence in Support of the Memorial to Congress "It was the last ounce that broke the back of the camel."

139. What is a broken friendship anyways? I don't think that's an actual term unless I just coined it. If that's the case, a proper definition should be given.

140. A Broken Friendship: (adj.)

1. A former friendship that crumbled, possibly as the result of broken promises, truth, and/or hearts.

2. Two friends who go off the side of a cliff together and break into a bunch of pieces as a result (see Thelma and Louise).

141. I read a list of the best breakup songs. Purple Rain (Prince) was listed as #1, followed by You Oughta Know (Alanis), I Can't Make You Love Me (Bonnie Raitt), I Will Always Love You (Dolly Parton), Ms. Jackson (OutKast), and Since You've Been Gone (Kelly Clarkson). Another list had I'd Rather Go Blind (Etta James) as #1, followed by Somebody that I Used to Know (Elliott Smith) as #2, and then the ones we've already seen with additions by Lauryn Hill, Smokey Robinson, Gladys Knight, and Adele. I continued to go through these lists. On average Taylor Swift seems to have the most entries. Frequently cited are: We Are Never Getting Back Together, All Too Well, and Dear John.

142. I was surprised to learn that breakup in the sense of "break it up" (meaning to stop fighting) came far later than its original use (to breakup groups, assemblies, marriages, etc.). The original use, as in our relationships, first came about in 1795. Break it up, to end a fight, came about in 1936.

143. People have been documenting breaking up since at least the 1700's and we still don't know how to do it right. We definitely know how to do it

wrong, but right? Not so much. Is there a proper way to break something?

144. I would have felt irresponsible writing this without diving into the antithesis of broke – what's unbroken or unbreakable. I was inevitably led to Louis Zamperini. His life is the subject of the book Unbroken, and the film version of the same title, directed by Angelina Jolie (see item #92). Zamperini faces undeniable adversities. When reading the book (written by Laura Hillenbrand), and watching the film, I was shaken and shocked by how much misfortune one man can have. He's a teenage Olympian, enlists, fights in WWII, his plane is shot down, he's stranded at sea on a raft for forty-six days, is captured, held in a camp, is brutally beaten and tortured almost daily, and stays that way for more than two years. A Japanese leader at the camp known as The Bird (Mutsuhiro Watanabe) really has it out for him, and takes great joy in making him suffer. Despite all of this, we are led to believe he remains "unbroken." To an extent, he does. The movie fails to mention his understandable PTSD and alcoholism after the war. So it seems he was broken after all. I think the implication of the film is that it's good to not let the world break you. However, in his case, it seems he

was broken. And that's okay. I wouldn't be alive let alone broken if I had endured what he did. I think I would have taken more from his brokenness had the film showed his post-war struggles, and his ability to overcome those despite his trauma.

145. He got sober. He remained happily married. He had children. In 1998, a few days before he turned 81, he flew to Japan. He ran part of the Olympic Torch relay, a few miles from where he had been held as a prisoner of war. During his time in Japan, he asked to meet with "The Bird." The Bird refused. So instead he sent him a letter saying he forgave him for the torture he inflicted on him during his time in the camp. The true story, the full story… the time between WWII and the 1998 Olympics show he was broken, but somehow he found a way to mend, enough so he could embrace Japan warmly, and forgive the man who broke him. That story is the one I needed to read in writing this. How did he fix what was broken? Unfortunately, I cannot ask him. He died in 2014 at the age of 97. The book focuses on his practice of Christianity, but I want to know specifically, what actions and practices helped.

146. Tylenol became commercially available in 1955. Although this was after WWII, I wonder if Zamperini took it often. If anyone needed to, surely it's him.

147. "Give me a break" became a popularized phrase when ET came out. There's a scene where Elliot says "Only little kids can see him" and Gertie, Drew Barrymore's character, responds with "give me a break." Every time I hear that phrase, I think of Drew. The phrase is still widely used today. Merriam Webster lists it in the top 7% of phrases used. I wonder if Drew Barrymore knows she has so much influence, it even sways the English dictionary. The actual origins of the phrase are unknown.

148. In the 1980's, musician Michael Levins wrote a jingle called Gimme a Break. You know it as the KitKat song. "Break me off a piece of that KitKat bar." The song has remained popular (perhaps not the right word) through the decades. In 2003, University of Cincinnati researcher James Kellaris named it one of the worst earworm offenders (songs that get stuck in your head). It's in the top ten. I'm not sure what number one is.

149. It's a clever tune. It uses the literal meaning of "break" as well as break in the sense of providing relief. It actually wasn't supposed to be the song used in the commercial. KitKat had picked a different song but wanted to show test groups two options. The test group overwhelmingly responded to "gimme a break." So blame them. Or take some Tylenol.

150. When I listen to the aforementioned metaphorically broken records, it's like listening to a literal broken record. The same memories play over and over in my head. A broken record sounds a lot like regret.

151. My elementary school had a large population of first generation Mexican-Americans. I heard the phrase "broken English" used as an adjective to describe their verbal communication frequently. Broken English is also a descriptor lazily used in texts that wish to exoticize a character. I've never cared much for either use. Especially as I've gotten older and traveled.

152. In New Zealand I learned the Māori often intentionally altered the English language to their liking (I'm not sure if they still do). They knew

"proper" English, but chose to make it their own. Language, like style, became part of their individuality. It was when I was laying on a beach outside of Takaka talking to a Kiwi (a white one) that I also learned the Māori aren't the only ones who did this. In Nigeria, broken English/Pidgin is widely spoken. It's spoken by roughly 75 million people. BBC News even offers the news in Pidgin. I read a few articles in it. I understood what they were saying with little effort. It has some altered spellings and doesn't use definite articles or verb tenses in the same way traditional English does. It was easier to wrap my head around than some Shakespeare.

153. Shakespeare used the term broken English, but in a completely different way than it is used today. From Henry V: "Come, your answer in broken music; for thy voice is music and thy English broken; therefore, queen of all, Katherine, break thy mind to me in broken English."

154. From BBC News Pidgin: "How south African mayor die two months after im predecessor die too."

155. Was Shakespeare or broken English easier for you to understand? Maybe that's why I don't like the term... because broken implies it is ruined or needs to be fixed. But if "broken English" needs to be corrected, then surely Shakespeare, and some other uses of the language need to be corrected too. I don't feel the urge to correct any of the above. They're all forms of communication to me – no lesser or more. And no need to fix. Each a mark of individuality.

156. There is a fantastic album by Marianne Faithful titled Broken English, named after one of the songs on the album. Marianne Faithful had been watching a documentary on Ulrike Meinhof and the Baader-Meinhof gang. Its subtitle said "broken English... spoken English." It intrigued her. "Don't say it in Russian/Don't say it in German/Say it in broken English." In the 60's Faithful was known for her soft, angelic voice. After the 60's, she fell heavily into addiction, ended up on the streets, and drank and smoked heavily. When she sobered up and reentered the public eye, she was harshly criticized for her now rough and raspy voice – almost sounding as if she was struggling for oxygen when speaking. I watched a documentary on her where people said her voice was considered

"ruined" and "broken" from years of substance abuse. Fortunately for us, she didn't give up. She used her new voice to create a new sound and released an album unlike anything ever recorded before, changing the recording industry for women. That album was Broken English. Sometimes, it's good to break things.

157. There is a movie from 1981 that gives nod to Pidgin. It's called Broken English. It's about a white woman who falls in love with a black South African freedom fighter. I suppose the movie maybe gave more attention to Pidgin outside of African knowledge. Although, I couldn't find any data to back this up.

158. There is a movie from 1996 that gives nod to the Māori version of broken English. It's called Broken English. It's about a white woman who falls in love with a Māori chef in New Zealand. I suppose the movie maybe gave more attention to the Māori version of the language outside of Kiwi knowledge. Although, I couldn't find any data to back this up.

159. I take another Tylenol. Two this time.

160. There is a movie from 2007 that gives nod to broken English in the general sense. It's called Broken English. It's about a white woman who falls in love with a French man who's white. I suppose the movie could've helped end the stigma of being uneducated when it comes to broken English, but probably not because people don't seem to have a problem when white foreigners speak broken English. Scrutiny is often reserved for nonwhite foreigners.

161. Whenever I speak broken Spanish abroad, it's met with smiles of encouragement for trying. What a difference.

162. Broken English just means you're bilingual. Something 80% of Americans are not.

163. The Broken English from 2007 isn't a bad movie. It has Parker Posey. I enjoyed it. I couldn't find copies of the other two titles.

164. I should review movies for a living.

165. "Mary praise the rosary for my broken mind." -Lana Del Rey

166. I was 13 when I realized all of you will die. Inevitable, I realized that one day I will also die. My

mind began to crack. I don't think this is when it broke completely, or even when it first started to erode. I think that happened much earlier. Around nine. That was when I first acknowledged suicide and didn't think it was the worst thing in the world. The thoughts about death don't make a person broken, it's how I responded to them. I began to obsess over them. There was a solid year, until I was fourteen where I never heard anyone, watched a movie, or listened to music. When I would try to have a conversation, or listen to music, or watch a film, all I could think was *this person is going to die. Are they scared? Do they know it? How will they die?* I would listen to The Beatles and instead of hearing the music, I would think *John is dead. George is dead. Were they scared? When will Paul and Ringo die? Are they scared?* I would watch a movie and the entire time think *What does Jennifer Aniston think will happen when we die? Will Nicole Kidman ever age? Is she scared of dying?* I don't remember a single thing from school that year. I barely slept at all. All I remember are those obsessive thoughts. I didn't tell anyone because being thirteen, I thought I was the first person ever in existence to have these thoughts. I didn't want to ruin anyone's life by putting dark thoughts in their head. I pictured myself in therapy and pictured my therapist promptly jumping out the window after our first session, or being unhappy for the rest of their life. The obsession is what broke my mind – not the initial thought. A broken mind seems to me now to just be a mind that cannot properly organize its thoughts anymore, whether because of the quantity or speed at which they enter.

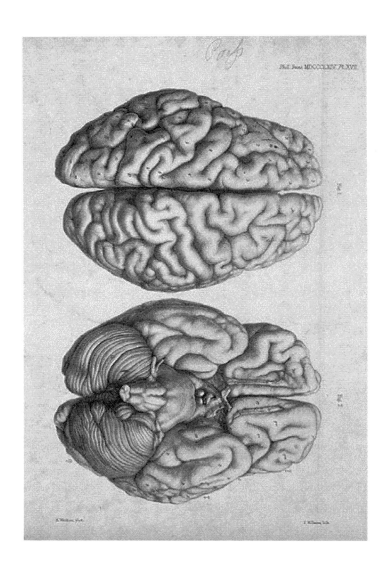

167. Maybe that's what broke us – not me, or us, or the thought of us even but my obsession. And admittedly, my obsession with you.

168. But us breaking broke me, or maybe just helped me to see the pieces that were already separated – like Pangea (see items #76-84).

169. Is obsession such a bad thing? Maybe it's just misunderstood, like the broken things.

170. On my birthday in 2015, Devon Welsh released his single Downtown as part of the group "Majical Cloudz." In it, he says "And if suddenly I die/I hope they will say/That he was obsessed and it was okay." He understood death and obsession, and discussed them in the same verse. My mind stopped racing.

171. I wondered if he understood what it is to be broken, and if maybe he is broken too, or if he ever has been. If being obsessed is a symptom of being broken, then surely he must be or must have been at some point. I scanned his catalogue for clues. In Heavy he wrote "So enamored I'm broken I feel it I am/But I know you hear me, you see me, you can/You gotta learn to love me."

172. The connotation here being we are broken and don't need fixing; we just have to learn to love the broken things.

173. Eventually there was a pill that aided my broken mind. While on it, I learned to train myself to not let obsession send me into episodes of panic and depression. I'm wondering if I can use my time now, on Tylenol, to train myself to not let the poking of these shards in my chest bother me.

174. In Gone with the Wind, Margaret Mitchell wrote "What's broken is broken, and I'd rather remember it as it was at its best than mend it and see the broken places as long as I live... I'm too old to believe in such sentimentalities as clean slates and starting all over." On one hand, Mitchell disagrees with Welsh: Mitchell arguing to remember broken things as they were and Welsh defending them, saying they should be loved as they are. However, they seem to agree there is no fixing them. At least Welsh alludes to this, while Mitchell blatantly says clean slates aren't real.

175. There is also the third, more terrifying possibility. I hadn't realized it until I read My Sister's Keeper. In it Jodi Picoult states "Lately, I've been having nightmares, where I'm cut into so

many pieces that there isn't enough of me to be put back together." Just like with broken bones, there are degrees to which our soul or heart can break. When we break to the degree in which the pieces are broken up so finely, part of ourselves becomes lost or nonexistent. It would seem we are only irreparable when we lose ourselves upon breaking. If we still know ourselves, perhaps there's hope. Or if we find ourselves, perhaps that's the path to healing.

176. There is a town in Nebraska called Broken Bow. It received its name from a settler who found a broken bow in a field when they settled. I was anticipating a story more exciting when I began looking into it.

177. There is a town in Oklahoma called Broken Bow. Perhaps the origin of its name is more exciting.

Herman Dierks

178. Broken Bow, OK was named by settlers Herman and Fred Dierks who moved to the area from Broken Bow, NE and named it after their hometown.

179. "But I felt that it was my heart which was broken. Something had broken in me to make me so cold and so perfectly still and far away." -James Baldwin. More symptoms of broken: cold and distant.

180. I had a phase of reading plays. The Glass Menagerie is a play by Tennessee Williams. In it, Williams writes "When you look at a piece of delicately spun glass you think of two things: how beautiful it is and how easily it can be broken." For months after reading this, I applied the lens to people: beautiful and easily broken. Williams frequently wrote of the broken and breakable things around us. Perhaps this was his fixation with Elizabeth Taylor, despite his homosexuality: a frequently shattered woman, who always managed to put the pieces back together.

181. Williams was influenced by Hart Crane who wrote The Broken Tower. "The bells, I say, the bells break down their tower; And swing I know not where. Their tongues engrave Membrane through marrow, my long-scattered score Of broken intervals... And I their sexton slave!"

182. The fixation on broken with both men seemed to be a reflection of their internal agony. Williams overdosed, Crane jumped off a boat.

183. I never got the impression in queer studies courses either man truly ever knew themselves. They came about at a very difficult time for homosexuals. It would be very hard to not be able to find the missing pieces when broken in those times.

184. I wondered if Margaret Mitchell was influenced by Goethe. She reminded me of something I read in Maxims and Reflections: "We look back on our life as a thing of broken pieces, because our mistakes and failures are always the first to strike us, and outweigh in our imagination what we have accomplished and attained." He and Mitchell seem to agree there is no clean slate. Perhaps this is true. I'm not sure it's true we see the broken pieces upon reflection always. Perhaps that's another symptom of being broken.

185. I found another town in Oklahoma that grabbed my attention: Broken Arrow. I hadn't received the exciting story I wanted from either Broken Bow town.

186. Broken Arrow was named after a community that lived on a creek in Alabama.

187. I have thrown my atlas away.

188. On a bus in New Zealand I passed by the Broken River, the Broken River Ski Area, and the Broken River Cave. I asked every person on the bus if they knew why everything had the word broken in the name. No one could tell me. I asked a group of Māori teens outside of Christchurch – they didn't know either. I considered asking if they had heard of broken English (and the form allegedly spoken by Māori people as a Pidgin language, but I was pressed for time) (see item #152).

189. There is a criminological theory called the Broken Window Theory. It was proposed in 1982 by James Q. Wilson and George L. Kelling. The theory states if there are broken windows, graffiti, etc. it will increase and encourage crime in the area. The theory was picked up by Rudy Giuliani when he was mayor of NYC. He ran with it and sold Times Square to Disney. This transaction led other conservative mayors in the US to believe the Broken Window Theory. However, studies done in recent years show examples used in earlier studies

were usually a result of mean reversion, and the drop in crime rate had less to do with aesthetic appeal and more to do with overall economic prosperity in the 90's after financial lows in the 80's. New York City remains a fairly safe city today, and still hosts its fair share of street art and broken windows.

190. Broken mirrors are blamed for bad luck, broken windows are blamed for crime, and broken hearts are blamed on you, and our broken relationship on me and my brokenness.

191. Broken mirrors and windows have largely been disproven as a culprit for bad – perhaps hearts will be vindicated next.

192. "I have seen the fracture of the human soul. So many broken lives, so much pain and anger, giving way to the poison of deep grief, until one crime became many." Hercule Poirot proclaims in Murder on the Orient Express. It seems he is also willing to blame problems on broken windows and broken people instead of asking if it's the problems with society that break the people, and not the people who break it. Perhaps it's both, a combination of warm and cool air creating the perfect tornado. A tornado moving through places like Broken Bow

and Broken Arrow, Oklahoma perhaps. Maybe finding the origin is fruitless, like asking if the chicken or egg came first. It doesn't matter how, it just matters that it is.

193. In 1866 nervous breakdown was used for the first time to describe a mental collapse (see item #166). In this case, we know whether it was the chicken or egg. People have been breaking down long before the English language or broken English was able to describe it. To break is as old as to be born.

193. I keep coming back to this though… that the only way to mend what's broken is to break further. Victor Hugo says in Les Misérables "The terrible shock of his sentence had in some way broken that wall which separates us from the mystery of things beyond and which we call life." His sentence broke a wall between life and mystery. That's what's trying to be achieved here: break the plaster between what's broken and mended, and make visible the path between the two.

194. I watched Nick and Norah's Infinite Playlist religiously when it came out, but didn't read the book until years later. When I did, I underlined an excerpt three times: "One part of Judaism called

tikkun olam. It says that the world has been broken into pieces. All this chaos, all this discord. And our job – everyone's job – is to try to put the pieces back together. To make things whole again... Maybe what we're supposed to do is come together. That's how we stop breaking." (See notes #76-84).

195. I was beside myself in astonishment for weeks after reading this. It encompasses so much of what has been written here, whether taken literally or metaphorically. From Pangea to broken people. It takes the etymology of broken and brings it to present day and offers a solution. Whether the solution be right or wrong, I'm unsure, but it offers one.

196. Tikkun olam means "world repair" in Hebrew. This dates back to 10-220 CE. The concept is meant to promote social welfare. This is often achieved through the performing of ritual mitzvot (good deeds). This suggests repairing what's broken is done through doing good.

197. I took this to mean doing good for others is how we repair ourselves and mend our own broken pieces.

198. Returning to broken bones… during the Covid-19 pandemic, a story was widely shared in which anthropologist Margaret Mead said the first signs of a developed society are a broken bone that's healed. This is because in the wild, an animal with a broken limb is usually left for dead. Healing indicates the person was cared for. In The Gift of Pain authors Philip Yancey and Paul W. Brand reported on the talk where she said this. She held a mended femur up and declared "Such signs of healing are never found among the remains of the earliest, fiercest societies." Our broken bones, broken hearts, and broken continents are as old as time. Mending what has been broken is a newer practice – although still old – where we acknowledge unraveling, and fix it.

199. I think the point of all of this, and my conclusion on all of the broken things, goes back to items #175 and #195. We're all going to break if we aren't already broken. The key to healing is more in not losing the pieces when we break: knowing who we are. At least that's the conclusion drawn from these fragments of broken things pieced together here on paper.

200. Breaking is engrained in us, healing isn't yet. It requires constant reminding.

201. I see the broken places and parts now. Maybe you just saw them sooner, and didn't know if and how these things could be repaired. I didn't either. I didn't even see them to begin with. We can't all be Margaret Mead.

202. I take another Tylenol, take my atlas out of the garbage, and look at routes to Broken Bow, OK.

"Well I never been to heaven/But I been to Oklahoma/Well they tell me I was born there/But I really don't remember." Three Dog Night

"The broken road/I set out on the narrow way/Many years ago/Hoping I would find true love/Along the broken road/I got lost a time or two/Wiped my brow, kept pushing through." Nitty Gritty Dirt Band

"When everything's meant to be broken, I just want you to know who I am" Goo Goo Dolls

Afterword

1. Break on Through (To the Other Side) is the first track on the first album by The Doors. Jim Morrison wrote the lyrics while walking across canals in Venice. The song is about breaking through mental barriers. When it was first recorded, the opening line was "she gets high," but that was scrapped because the record company thought it would limit radio play. They broke through the music industry with the song, a billboard on Sunset BLVD featured the band and proclaimed "The Doors break on through with an electrifying album." It was the first album I bought post puberty, and it broke through my mind. That's where my obsession with broken things comes from. I have been highlighting the word in text since. Jim had an obsession with it too, saying in 1966 about his songwriting "I like ideas about breaking away." It's mostly what he wrote about. Break on Through was the last song The Doors ever performed live before Jim Morrison broke on through to the other side. He's buried in Paris.

2. I pulled out some of my broken records when I finished writing this (see item #134). When I informed some of these people I was writing about

them, it wasn't met with anger like I expected. We dip our toes in, we say hello. It's a start. Maybe we can't go back to the records we used to listen to, but maybe we will find another, together.

I went to see Jim's grave in 2018. I climbed over the fence around it at sunrise and laid on top listening to "Break on Through" and "The End." I teared up before I saw myself being photographed by other tourists. I wish I could say I broke through and felt some sort of presence, but that would be a lie. It was just incredibly upsetting. I'm still glad I went though.

Consultations

20th Century Women (2016)

"The Origin of Continents" Alfred Wegener

"Only Women Bleed" Alice Cooper

"Cecilia and the Satellites" Andrew McMahon in the Wilderness

Angie (1994)

"Walking on Broken Glass" Annie Lennox

"Blackbird" The Beatles

"For Emma" Bon Iver

Broken English (1981)

Broken English (1996)

Broken English (2007)

"A Peculiar Treasure" Edna Ferber

"In Praise of the Broken Home" Ellen Lupton

E.T. (1982)

"Sonnet of the Garland of Roses" Federico Garcia Lorca

"Gabriel" George Sand

"Maxims and Reflections" Goethe

"The Broken Tower" Hart Crane

"Maimonides and the Biblical Prophets" Israel Drazin

"Breakdown" Jack Johnson

"Broken" Jack Johnson

"A Million Little Pieces" James Frey

"My Sister's Keeper" Jodi Picoult

"Unbroken" Lauren Hillenbrand

"Anna Karenina" Leo Tolstoy

"Hard Out Here" Lily Allen

"Downtown" Majical Cloudz

"Heavy" Majical Cloudz

"The Red Fighter Pilot: The Autobiography of the Red Baron" Manfred von Richthofen

"Gone with the Wind" Margaret Mitchell

"Broken English" Marianne Faithful

"Can Tylenol Help Heal a Broken Heart?" Melissa Hill

Murder on the Orient Express (2017)

Practical Magic (1998)

"Broken Glass" Rachel Platten

"Fight Song" Rachel Platten

"A Defense of Superstition." Robert Lynd

"No, Tylenol Won't Heal Your Broken Heart, But This Might…" Samier Mansur

Split (2016)

"State of Grace" Taylor Swift

"The Glass Menagerie" Tennessee Williams

Trudell (2005)

"Les Misérables" Victor Hugo

Unbroken (2014)

"I'm Fat" Weird Al Yankovic

"Henry V" William Shakespeare

"Richard II" William Shakespeare

"The Gift of Pain" Philip Yancey and Paul W. Brand

Acknowledgements

Joe Brainard, Maggie Nelson, Patti Smith, and Ali Liebegott for showing the formatting ways

All of the broken consultants

And even you for the shards

Made in the USA
Monee, IL
18 March 2022

ff5ce717-9db0-44e8-8260-064e75472e43R02